Turid Rugaas

What Do I Do...

... When My Dog Pulls?

Published by Qanuk Ltd
2004

Author: Turid Rugaas
Boks 109, 3361 Geithus, Norway
Tel: + 47 32 78 09 87 Email: turidrug@frisurf.no
Website: www.turidrugaas.com

Photographs by: Turid Rugaas, Kirsten Berger, Gerd Köhler,
Animal Learn and Sheila Harper
Written in English by Turid Rugaas
Edited by Sheila Harper

Title of the original Norwegian version:
Hva gjør jeg når hunden drar i båndet?

First published in Norway in 2003
First published in English in 2004

Published by: Qanuk Ltd
9 The Meadows,
Rugeley,
Staffs WS15 1JH
Registered in England No: 4998007

Printed by The Benhill Press Ltd.

ISBN no: 0-9548032-0-5

Contents

Foreword

Sometimes I admire people.

I had a pupil and her dog coming towards me in a very unusual way some winters ago. Down the hill at full speed came the owner sitting on the ground, legs stretched out in front of her, holding on to the leash of a very happy Bernese Mountain Dog. He had a smile all over his face and was galloping towards me very quickly, ears flapping and zest for life written all over him.

The owner was not quite so happy, and was relieved when the dog stopped. She had had absolutely no chance of standing on her feet on the icy road, and so they made this spectacular entrance.

I like to help such great people and their dogs to be able to cope with whatever they encounter, and that is why I love the method I finally decided upon for walking with a dog on a slack leash. It really is a great tool for helping people to control the situation in a nice way.

How it all began...

Over the years I have asked the pupils coming to my classes what they wanted to teach their dogs. The answer that topped the list was "to walk nicely on leash".

Next on the list were "to stop jumping on people", "to come when called" followed by a variety other things. However, walking nicely was definitely the winner.

Very understandable! I can't think of anything more annoying than walking a dog that is pulling away or lunging at dogs and bicycles. It can also be quite dangerous.

One winter some years ago, it was icy everywhere. It was difficult to stand up in the icy conditions and virtually impossible to hold dogs if they were pulling on leash. People were frequently falling over and breaking their bones. It was then that I made up my mind to look into and develop a method for teaching dogs to walk nicely on a loose leash and to prevent pulling if the dog were to forget to keep the leash slack. Of course dogs can forget even if they have learnt something well – we all forget sometimes. Dogs are no different from us in this way.

I wanted to find a kind method, one that did not hurt, frighten or stress the dogs – and most of the methods I had seen until then were not gentle.

I got the chance a little later whilst attending a one-year instructor course at Groruddalen Veterinary Clinic outside Oslo. We were asked to choose project work for the year, and being a practical person I, of course, had to pick a practical project. I chose to develop a method for teaching dogs to walk nicely on leash.

It turned out to be great fun. I advertised for "guinea pigs" and received 204 replies right away: people who had dogs with a variety of pulling problems. The youngest was a collie pup of four months of age; the oldest a Norwegian Elkhound who was 14 years old.

All kinds of breeds, all ages and types of dogs were represented, along with all kinds of pulling problems.

To make the project work possible and to get some valid results, I had to make the study rigid. Statistics are important to people, and I needed results that could be used and referred to.

In its simplicity I wanted to try out the following:

- ignoring any unwanted behaviour by standing still whenever the dog pulled on leash

- doing nothing apart from preventing the dog from being able to pull

- praising and rewarding the dog for walking nicely with the handler

In order to get valid results we chose one particular stretch of road and counted every time the dog made the leash tight.

The method was very simple, and quite inflexible – it has developed further and has been modified since then as I will show later.

Every dog taking part in the project was represented by its own graphic curve where the number of times it had pulled on the leash was marked each day, from day 1 to day 30. When everything was finished there were 196 curves, one for each dog finishing the project. They were so alike that I could have laid them on top of each other and made a carbon copy of the first one!

Then I made an average graph, which looked like this:

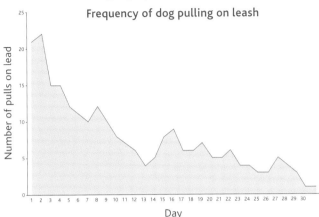

Frequency of dog pulling on leash

Number of pulls on lead

Day

On average there were more than 70 pulls on leash on the first day. After 30 days the average number of pulls on the same stretch of road had dropped to only one, and that pull was barely noticeable.

After this project I was sure I was on the road to success. However, I had to adjust the method a little. I would have to start off by making it easier for the dogs to avoid becoming stressed, and making it easier for people to learn how to do it.

Little by little I tried out and developed my technique until I had refined it so well that it has become the method I use today. I have taught it to people all over the world, and now feel satisfied with it. It is simple enough for everybody to be able to use with the minimum of help and explanation, and it is also simple enough for dogs to learn quickly.

The feedback I receive is sometimes almost ecstatic, such as:

> "*I just* LOVE *that leash work of yours!*"

I am happy about this, as it often means a better life for a dog.

Let's look at this method now.

The Basic Method

Let's look at this method as if it were a recipe. We need to be aware of the following:

Ingredients

> One dog
> One person
> Harness or soft collar
> Leash
> Treats

Method – the short version

Teach the dog to respond to a signal, for example clicking with your tongue.

- 🐾 **STOP** immediately the leash becomes tight or is about to tighten

- 🐾 **WAIT** two seconds – stand still – say nothing

- 🐾 **MAKE** a clicking or smacking sound with the tongue or lips

When the dog starts to turn his head towards you:

- 🐾 **PRAISE** him

- 🐾 **WALK** a couple of steps in another direction and the dog will follow

- 🐾 **REWARD** the dog for following

Repeat every time you want to change direction, or whenever the dog is about to pull.

Stop when the dog pulls

Make your sound

Reward the dog for his response

5

Even if someone or something is a distraction this method works well

Stop when the dog pulls

Make your sound

Walk away in the opposite direction with the dog following and reward

Working Manual

How to train your dog to walk without pulling

A leash is not necessary for the first three steps.

Step 1 – Teach the dog a simple neutral sound (clicking with the tongue, or patting your thigh), which means only one thing: "Follow me".

Teach it in this way:

- 🐾 Start inside or in a quiet place without distractions
- 🐾 Have the dog fairly close and have a treat ready in your hand
- 🐾 Use the sound you have decided to teach the dog
- 🐾 The dog will turn towards the sound: dogs being naturally curious want to investigate new sounds
- 🐾 The second the dog turns towards the sound, praise and treat him
- 🐾 Repeat this a few times and he will soon learn that the sound indicates a treat or something pleasant

The dog has now learnt that at the signal he should turn to you for a reward.

Step 2

- 🐾 Remain in a quiet place
- 🐾 Make the sound
- 🐾 Praise the dog when he turns towards you, and move a few steps away from the dog
- 🐾 He will follow to get his reward

The dog has now learnt to follow you to get a reward.

Step 3

- Ensure that there are still no distractions
- Make the sound
- Praise the dog when he turns towards you
- Take a few steps (just 2 – 3 steps to begin with or the dog will become frustrated and give up)
- Reward the dog when he follows
- Make the sound again and change direction
- Repeat this between three to five times in a row
- Walk in a different direction each time; praise and treat your dog when he follows you

The dog has now learnt to follow you and walk with you wherever you go when you give him the signal.

Step 4

- Continue to work in a place with no distractions
- The next step is to use a leash (not an extendable leash) and to do exactly the same as before
- Always have a completely slack leash. Be aware of your hand and ensure you don't pull or put any pressure at all on the leash

The dog has now learnt to follow you on a loose leash.

Step 5

- Continue to work somewhere with no distractions
- Now you can gradually start to increase the difficulty of the exercise

- 🐾 Walk a few steps further each time
- 🐾 Change direction frequently

The dog is now learning to walk on a loose leash in a variety of places.

Gradually increase the amount of time you practise with your dog from a couple of minutes to five minutes, then ten minutes and possibly more if your dog is able to concentrate for this length of time.

If your dog loses concentration it is because he is tired. It is likely that you have worked for too long. You cannot force anyone to concentrate: you probably realise this from your own experience. The ability to concentrate can vary with age, stress and previous working experience.

Step 6 – Increase the difficulty little by little by introducing distractions.

Distractions can be:

- 🐾 cars at a little distance, moving increasingly closer until you can finally walk along a road where there is traffic.
- 🐾 bicycles
- 🐾 children on roller skates
- 🐾 cats
- 🐾 horses, cows and other livestock
- 🐾 children playing football

Always start with the distractions at a distance and gradually move closer as long as the dog is coping well with them.

Step 7 – Start giving treats a little less: every second or third time, gradually decreasing the frequency with which they are offered. Vary how you use the treats, but never stop using them completely as your dog will need a reward now and again. However, you can tell him that you are pleased with him.

By doing this systematically, you will soon have a dog that walks nicely most of the time. If you are consistent, this learning is for life.

With a little consistent training...

your dog will find it much easier to walk past anyone approaching

Why do dogs pull on leash?

When you are hanging onto a pulling dog, feeling that your arms are coming out of their sockets, or when the dog suddenly lunges at a passing bicycle, making you fly through the air, it is no fun walking him.

So, the question is, why do dogs do this? It must be unpleasant and painful for them too.

Unpleasant and uncomfortable – something neither you nor your dog will enjoy

or ...

... a pleasant walk with your dog along the road, in the woods or in town. Could anything be more enjoyable?

Yes, it is both unpleasant and painful, but remember that dogs think differently from us. They make direct associations, and are unable to consider consequences in the same way that we can. We need to start thinking about how dogs learn, and how they form associations in their minds.

Fig. 11

When the dog chooses to go somewhere we often follow

Let's look at a variety of reasons for pulling

1. The dog pulls because when he does so, you follow.

   In other words: **you must not follow!**

2. You have previously taught your dog by using corrections. The dog has learnt to pull because of the timing of your correction:

   The dog pulls ...

   ... you decide to teach him not to pull by jerking or checking on the leash.

   To be able to jerk or check you have to slacken the leash for a moment.

Then comes the jerk or check. For the dog, this means pain, and he learns that the slackening of the leash means that pain will follow.

Your dog will now try to avoid the loose leash in order to avoid the pain that he knows will follow, and consequently he is even more likely to pull on leash.

3. Walking on leash hurts his neck. He finds it difficult to breathe due to the tight collar, so he tries to escape by getting as far away as possible.

4. You are using an extendable leash, which is designed to always be taut. Whatever the dog tries to do, the leash is always tight and makes him feel uncomfortable. The dog gives up trying to keep a slack leash.

5. You are irritable. You often yell at the dog, grabbing him by the neck or anything else that is unpleasant – so the dog tries to get as far away as he can – pulling away from your side.

   In other words: stop being the one the dog wants to keep away from. No worthwhile relationship can come of this, and he won't learn to walk comfortably with you either.

6. Your dog generally has too high a stress level. It will make him much more active and erratic and he will have a hard time walking more slowly and concentrating on what he is doing.

When we look at the different reasons for pulling, let's consider the following points:

- **Do not let** your dog pull you. Stop. Stand still.
- **Help** your dog to do the right thing and praise and reward him for it.

13

🐾 **Build** a bond with your dog. Build up a good relationship and then you will have few problems wherever you walk with him.

🐾 **Avoid** health problems: avoid jerking and pulling, both of which cause injuries and which can often damage the thyroid gland, the neck and the back.

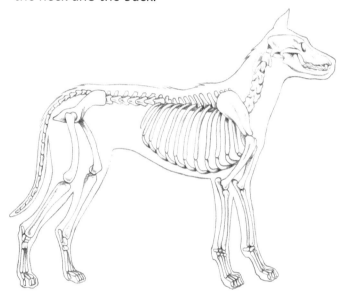

One hard jerk on a leash, or many small ones can easily damage your dog's skeleton or other parts of the body. It can also potentially cause blindness or poor sight – and possibly brain damage. Whiplash damage is not uncommon.

This is something to bear in mind. Use a well-fitting harness instead of a collar. Stop jerking and pulling the dog, and do not allow yourself to follow the dog when he pulls. These are simple remedies for better health for many dogs.

Troubleshooting

- If the dog seems to get stressed you must look more closely at what you are doing. Are you standing too long so the dog turns to go back to you? Walk on quickly in another direction, so the dog does not have to be like a yoyo.

- Does the dog move towards you to get into the heel position? Once again, you are waiting too long, so start moving away from the dog.

- Don't teach your dog to make eye contact in any of these phases of training. If you do this he will learn to make eye contact, and he won't be able to concentrate on what you really intend him to learn: walking on a loose leash.

- Does the dog take the treat and move off again? Then you should pause before you give him the treat, just giving him praise. Then reward him, turn and change direction more frequently in order to make it more interesting for him to follow you.

- Is the dog a bit erratic in his movements? Walk much more slowly yourself, as if you were out strolling along looking at the scenery. Relax! Have a nice time! Don't rush – otherwise your dog will be inclined to do the same.

- Does the dog refuse treats? This is likely to be because he is stressed. Perhaps you should work on your dog's stress levels first. Maybe you need to use better treats, or perhaps you are still a bit "dominant" or too demanding in your voice and body language.

Perhaps your dog refuses treats because there are too many distractions. If so, find a quieter place. There is always a reason for a dog not taking treats, so try to find out what this might be. Change the environment or your approach to the dog.

If your dog is very interested in his surroundings you will be more successful if you move to a place with fewer distractions

🐾 Ensure that the dog does not have a health problem that causes discomfort. There may be pain in his hips, legs or back or there may be some other problem.

Perhaps your dog does not respond to the signal for following you? Dogs become "deaf" when they are stressed, so again you will have to look for causes of stress. Don't get angry as your dog can't help it.

🐾 Does your dog bite the leash or your trouser legs? This will also be a symptom of stress. A young dog is likely to behave like this when he gets tired or excited. Young dogs can easily get tired when the walk is a little too long. He might get excited when there is too much happening around him, or perhaps the owner is nagging him too much.

Tugging on leash can be a learnt behaviour but is often a sign of tiredness, stress or over-excitement

🐾 If the dog doesn't seem to hear you when you make the sound because he is too interested in looking or sniffing at something, just WAIT. Stand still and relax. It is a fact that when a dog uses one sense, he literally cuts out another. So when he concentrates on sniffing something of interest, he does not hear. Therefore just wait a few seconds before you try again, and usually he will respond perfectly.

🐾 Remember that for a dog it is much more important to use his senses and to avoid conflicts than to be obedient. To a dog, obedience has no value. He will do things to please us or to get something he wants, but it will be a learnt behaviour and will have nothing to do with what he really needs to do.

* If you get a poor response to your "follow me" signal, it might be that you are waiting too long. Give the signal as early as possible. Don't wait until the dog is already starting to eat the Sunday roast! Make your neutral sound when it seems as if he is intending to go in the wrong direction, or has just started to move. Give this signal the second he looks as if he intends to run up to a child or a person who is unlikely to want him jumping up them. Don't wait until he is already jumping all over someone!

Giving an early warning is much fairer to the dog, and it will be so much easier for him to respond to you.

* Do not make it too difficult for him to respond to the sound. There is nothing that can destroy good training more than demanding too much of a dog. Think about how you feel yourself when you have demands made on you that you can't live up to. Nothing ruins your self-esteem more than that.

* Perhaps your dog makes progress with the leash training initially and then seems to deteriorate?

If so, you might be training for too long a period of time. Have short sessions in the beginning, not more than 10 minutes, possibly less. Then you can lengthen the training sessions little by little.

Gentle walks are a pleasure for both owner and dog

Not only should sniffing be allowed, it is essential for your dog's mental health

Which is the most suitable equipment to use?

Harness   This takes pressure off the neck and is much more comfortable for the dog. (See fig. 1)

It should not be one of those harnesses designed to cause discomfort such as one that tightens when the dog begins to pull. (See fig. 6)

Collar   This should be one made of broad, soft material. You can even get them padded with quilted material. Dogs seem to feel more comfortable in them.

However, for the vast majority of dogs harnesses are still the best, because they lessen neck pressure and the danger of whiplash when sudden pressure occurs.

The collar should have no choking (checking) effect and should not be a half-choke / half-check.

Leash   This should be an ordinary 2 – 3 metre long soft leather leash, or a leash made of cotton webbing. These are easy to adjust from long to short when needed. (See fig. 2)

The most simple equipment is always the best. The more equipment you try to use when training the easier it is for things to go wrong.

Fig. 1

Body harnesses are comfortable for dogs, avoiding pressure around the neck

Fig. 2

A long leash means that the dog can move around. When not in use a leash like this can be folded up in the hand

Equipment to be avoided, and why

🐾 Head halters and similar equipment that are placed around the dog's head. (Fig. 3)

Fig. 3

Not only is a head halter uncomfortable but it prevents the dog from signalling to other dogs and may put him at risk

Why? Because it is very uncomfortable to be pulled around by the head. Try it yourself and you will realise how restricting it is.

It also prevents the dog from looking around, choosing where to look and sniff, and giving signals to other dogs. It is important for his own safety that the dog is allowed to do these things.

Most dogs also become depressed, and it is easy to see this just by looking at them. Others might become irritable at this thing around their face that can also touch their eyes when they are ill fitting. If they are tight it can make it hard for them to breathe normally. An irritable or depressed dog does not enjoy walks and can become stressed. Other, more deep-rooted problems may then occur.

🐾 Pinch collars. (Fig. 4)

Why? Because they hurt! Try to wear one yourself. It really causes a lot of pain, and if you look under the fur you will clearly see bruising, with red, sore skin.

Fig. 4

A pinch or prong collar causes a lot of pain

We should not cause a dog pain just because we can't be bothered to work through the problem of pulling.

❧ Check chains or check collars, either of metal, leather or any other material or design that can choke the dog or tighten around his throat. (Fig. 5)

Fig. 5

Check chains frequently damage the dog's neck and windpipe

Why? Because dogs choke when they are used and have to gasp for air. Besides being uncomfortable and painful, collars such as these also hurt and damage the dog's neck. Dogs are unable to get enough oxygen, and also the blood circulation is interrupted. Some veterinarians have suggested that blindness and poor eyesight in dogs might come from equipment hindering blood circulation to the head.

Another serious effect is that when the dogs feel they are being choked or feel neck pain from jerking, they associate this pain directly with whatever they are focused on, another dog or a human. This is the most frequent cause of a dog learning to be fearful or aggressive towards other dogs or people.

❧ "Walk–nicely" harnesses that are designed to tighten when the dog pulls. (Fig. 6)

Fig. 6

This kind of harness is uncomfortable and can give your dog the wrong associations with his environment

Why? For the reasons mentioned above. They cause pain, restricting the dog's movements, and are likely to cause the dog to associate the pain and discomfort with whatever he is focused on at that time.

I have actually treated dogs for fear of this type of harness. Their fear was so bad that they screamed and tried to hide when the owner wanted to put them on the dog. When you think about how much dogs love to go out, this kind of reaction should tell you something about how painful these kinds of harnesses are to use.

🐾 Very short leashes.

Why? Because a short leash will restrict the dog's movements so much that he will not be able to walk freely, look around or sniff, and he will have a constant pressure on the throat and neck.

I see dogs on these very short leashes occasionally. The dogs' faces and eyes show signs of depression, fear and sometimes even despair.

🐾 Water squirt bottles.

Why? Mostly because of the effect of learning by this method. Dogs, like all living creatures, learn by association. They learn to associate the unpleasant, startling squirt of water with you, with your hand movement, with a place or whatever the dog is focussed on at that point in time. Many people imagine that dogs learn not to pull when they use this water squirt. In a very few cases the dogs may learn this, but personally I have **never** seen them learn what is intended. Usually they will learn to be afraid of something quite different.

For example: one dog I saw learnt not to pull **only** when the trainer was present.

Another dog learnt to become afraid of water and consequently hid whenever he heard running water or when his owner turned on a tap.

If the dog stops pulling (or barking or lunging) when he is squirted with water it is not because he has learnt what you intended. Instead it is because he is startled with the sudden splash of water in his face. You would also be likely to stop talking or whatever you were doing if someone threw something at you or squirted water at you. But does that mean that you had learnt not to talk as a result? Of course not – you stopped only because of the startling effect of the water spray.

🐾 Anything at all that is used to cause pain or discomfort to the dog.

Why? Because we have no right in our human arrogance to cause pain when it can so easily be avoided.

Puppies

Puppies need time to explore their surroundings on a slack leash. This method is easy to train when you start early

The learning rules for puppies will be a little different than those for adult dogs.

Puppies can concentrate for seconds only, and you can't force a puppy to work for longer than he is able. Do remember that puppies are babies and even if they seem big and capable, they are not. Not yet.

How do I train a puppy to walk without pulling?

Start training the puppy during the first week by letting him get used to a collar, harness and leash. Put each piece of equipment gently on the puppy, and let him have it on for a short while, under supervision, so that he doesn't get tangled up in anything.

Next teach the puppy the neutral sound (see step 1 on page 7) which will become a signal for attention.

Repeat a few times each day and the puppy will quickly

learn this.

Use the attention signal to help the puppy move away from mischief or investigation of things you do not want him to investigate. Use the signal before he has the opportunity to do the wrong thing.

Also be sure that you do not do this all the time, or it will become like nagging the puppy, and it will only make him unsure and stressed. Move things out of reach for a while! Make the house puppy proof. This is much better than running around getting irritated and making the puppy unhappy, frustrated and possibly afraid, and it will only be for a short time. In a matter of months most things in the household will be able to return to normal.

When the puppy knows the signal for attention, start walking around the living room with him for 10-15 seconds. When he follows readily, put a leash on him, making sure the leash is totally loose when you work with him. Very short sessions and prompt rewards are most effective. Change directions frequently.

You can also start using the sound for recalls at a short distance away from the puppy. We need to call puppies at very short distances anyway: between two to three metres in the beginning, increasing the distance as they grow older.

If you start training the puppy like this, he will be able to walk nicely with you as he grows up. Puppies should have only very short walks in the beginning, maybe 10 minutes at three months of age, adding five minutes each month, which means he will have normal length walks when he reaches adult age.

He will also have learnt to walk nicely on a leash!

Teaching the adult and the older dog

There is no age limit for learning. Although youngsters learn quickly, they also forget quickly and they need frequent repetition. Older dogs learn just as quickly, and new things usually stay with them almost at once. They are able to concentrate better, and have enough life experience to see the value of being treated nicely.

I actually love having older dogs for training; it's wonderful to see how well they understand when you "explain" things to them.

Whatever their age, dogs with a chasing instinct respond equally well to this technique

Example 1:

A nine-year-old Labrador bitch was pulling so badly that her whole chest was on the ground, and her wheezy breathing was terrible to listen to. Shortly prior to this the owner had developed such bad tendon problems that she had to give up work. Since the pulling was the cause of the problem, she was told to get rid of the dog. She decided to try training first and she called me.

The first lesson with this dog was memorable. I had to use all my skills to be able to hold her, but within a few moments she had learnt what I wanted to teach her to do, and did it happily. It felt so much better for her too, of course.

A couple of weeks later she came for her second lesson, and it was like a parade: she was walking like an angel beside her owner on a totally loose leash, looking contented and happy.

The Labrador continued to walk nicely on leash for the rest of her life. I saw her with her owner now and again in the village, and she never ever pulled again.

An older dog knows when something becomes better. It was simply that she had never had the chance to learn this before!

Example 2:

Something similar happened to a 13 year old Golden Retriever who came to see me. Not because the owner wanted to do any training with him, or thought he could teach his dog anything at that age. He came because he was curious to see how I worked with dogs, and which methods I used.

I spent just a few minutes with the dog, who became tired very easily as he had never done anything before, and because he was old. After 8-10 minutes of a little simple training, we stopped and strolled back to the car. He walked on a loose leash, and actually looked at his owner now and again.

The owner was shocked, and didn't say anything until he was about to set off in his car. Then he turned around and said: "This is the first time in his whole life that my dog has looked at me when we are out together."

Old dogs learn, and learn quickly. And it stays with them. Just remember that they also get tired quickly. Short, pleasant sessions are the best way to train them.

Praise the behaviour you
require and your dog will
soon be walking nicely

Using the technique in class

You can also use this method in class situations of course.

If the dogs are excited let them have some space or have fewer working together at the same time, for example. However, this method can work really well in groups too.

Once the dogs have been trained in the initial steps of walking without pulling, it can be a good idea to make exercises a little more varied. Have fun, or a little competition, or find some other practical ways of training.

Exercises

1. Place two objects about five – six metres apart.

   Practise leash work by walking in a figure 8 around the two objects. These can be anything from chairs to buckets, hats, or even stones.

   Vary the objects from time to time in order to make it more interesting.

2. Place five or six objects in a row and weave between them with your dog. To increase the difficulty you can hold a plastic beaker full of water in the same hand as the leash. You can also use a spoon with a potato, mushroom or a hardboiled egg in it, for example.

3. Practise having your dog pass people and objects. Let a person walk towards the dog and owner, with the owner working on giving the signal early enough, and passing in a curve.

4. Place many different objects all over the floor (hoola hoops, chairs, balls, doll's pram, bags, kettle, shoes...) and let the handlers and dogs weave their way from one end to the other.

5. If you want to make it a competition, you can deduct points for touching objects with feet and paws.

6. Practise with a bicycle passing slowly while the dogs go past nicely with a loose leash.

Use your creativity and find exercises that will help people to be good at handling the leash correctly, and be able to keep their dogs with them in all situations.

Using the technique in everyday life

Think about all the things for which you can use this technique: walking your dog, handling it at home or out and about, wherever you go.

At home for example, you could use it when the dog wants to go over to a guest, especially if the guest is afraid of dogs. You can give the signal for paying attention and get the dog back to you.

Your dog is running happily towards a child. You can stop him in the same way without giving the dog the wrong association by telling him not to do so. The signal for paying attention is not negative, and you should not sound angry.

A situation could arise where someone has opened the door and the dog is almost out of the door. By using the signal you can make the dog come right back to you without you getting angry or scaring the dog.

Situations like these can frequently happen. Simply make your sound and encourage your dog to move away from distractions

There are many ways of using this technique whilst out on a walk. As the same signal is given all the time it becomes easy to remember even in a crisis, and is something you begin to do automatically.

Imagine that some walkers are coming towards you in the forest. You can easily make the dog follow you and pass them in a curve.

Perhaps a cyclist is coming at full speed. You can respond quickly getting your dog out of the way by giving the signal as soon as you notice the cyclist and then moving out of the way yourself. No tight leashes, and no startling things should happen to make the dog react.

Few dogs can ignore shopping bags full of good food. Be aware of distractions you pass and help your dog follow you instead

You might see something like a half-eaten hot dog lying on the pavement. When you discover it, you can easily help your dog to pass it.

You pass a garden post, and your dog is starting to lift his leg – but since people do not like their fences and gates to be urinated on you can quickly use the signal to move the dog away from it to a safer place.

A group of school children come towards you yelling and shouting and taking up most of the pavement. You can take your dog past them in a curve, walking a little out into the street or to the other side. All the time you can praise and treat your dog who can walk past with all this noise around.

Gradually get your dog used to distractions and he'll be able to walk nicely in many situations

In other words, you can use this technique for a lot of things in daily life, without getting angry or giving the dog any wrong ideas.

Try it, and you will find how easy and useful it is.

It also makes life easier for us, since we do not need to remember a lot of different commands and messages.

Using this technique when bicycles are passing will help your dog cope much more easily

Use your sound to encourage the dog to curve away, passing with no problem

Meeting other dogs doesn't have to be a problem

People you walk with can even be a barrier to help your dog pass others more easily

Some tempting
food on the ground

I can pass that!

When you should NOT use this technique

- 🐾 Until your dog has learnt this technique really well and is highly skilled at walking on a loose leash most of the time, you should not try to make him walk nicely on his way to the park where he has a lot of fun, or to other places where he is really keen to go.

This would be far too much to demand of a dog.

- 🐾 You cannot expect a dog to be able to do this for the entirety of a long walk, either. In the beginning, five to ten minutes will make the dog very tired from the concentration of working. With practice, he will be able to concentrate for longer and longer. When he is quite good at walking nicely and following your attention signal, you might practise for a whole walk. However, if your dog becomes tired, stressed or starts biting the leash or barking at other dogs – or any of the other things dogs do when they become stressed - you have overdone the training session, and the dog will be incapable of learning any more.

In the cases where you cannot use the training techniques, but have to walk the dog, you can do any of the following:

- 🐾 Sit down and have a rest

- 🐾 Let the dog off leash (not always possible, of course)

- 🐾 Change to another leash, or from the collar to a harness, and then allow the dog to pull. You will soon find out that he doesn't pull as hard as he used to.

🐾 Walk back and forth, or in a direction that is not so interesting

🐾 For a short stretch you can hold a treat in your hand, and hold your hand either:

a) by your hip, where you want the dog to walk

b) where the dog can see it.

🐾 Walk backwards (not all places are suitable for this!) – hold your hand with a treat at the front of your body at about waist level, and the dog will follow in front of you.

Try walking backwards – your dog should follow

Remember: When the dog is very stressed, excited or afraid it is no use even trying to train. Find another time and place to do it. When stress levels become high, the brain doesn't function so well, and the dog literally can not hear or concentrate on anything.

Why negatives should not be used

I have already mentioned that health is at risk by using collars if the dog pulls or is being jerked about. Since so many dogs have back and neck problems, and since it is possible to crush the thyroid gland, this is something that should seriously be taken into consideration.

Another serious consequence is that dogs may learn the wrong association.

By being angry or using other negative signals it is very likely that the dog may become nervous, stressed or frustrated which will not help him at all in getting him to walk nicely.

The dog can even become afraid of you, his owner, which can of course become a real problem.

But the most obvious consequence is that all too often dogs get the wrong association towards other dogs and people, and this often leads to negative behaviour such as "aggression".

A dog that is jerked on leash is not only unable to communicate properly but health and behaviour problems all too frequently occur as a result

Learning by association

It is a well-known fact that dogs **learn by association**. We learnt this from Ivan Pavlov more than a hundred years ago, and yet we have still not learnt to use this knowledge properly.

It works like this:

Your dog is focused on something, such as a dog (as they very often are), a person, a child or an object.

Whilst he is focused something scary, painful, or anything negative happens (for example: you yell, you say "NO" in an angry voice, you jerk on the leash, you pinch the dog's ear...). In most cases the dog will associate what he is focused on with the negative message.

Now your dog is much more likely to become afraid of the dog, person or child he is focused on, unsure about them, or angry towards them ("aggressive"), as he views them as the cause of this pain or your anger.

This negative influence can often happen by accident, such as when something just happens to fall on the dog whilst he is looking at something else, or if he gets an electric shock having accidentally touched an electric fence whilst looking at horses in a field. This kind of experience can happen to all of us.

Or it can be that we purposely say "no" to something, and after a while the dog learns to think about it as dangerous. Sometimes people jerk the leash to try to teach the dog not to pull, and as a result the dog becomes aggressive with other dogs, simply because he was looking at another dog when there was a jerk on the leash.

A tight leash can
cause problems...

... dogs are less able
to effectively
communicate with
others when the
leash is tight

We **have** to remind ourselves all the time that dogs' minds work this way. Most problem behaviours relate to some negative association.

If we understand how this works, we will never need to have a dog who becomes frightened of or aggressive towards people or dogs, children, bicycles or anything else.

But let us look at a few cases where association has played a large role:

1. A little Basenji puppy was brought home by a wife to her anxiously waiting husband. The kitchen door opened, and at the same moment that the puppy saw the man standing in the room, a broomstick fell on her. She became terrified of the husband, and when the couple came to me 1 $1/2$ years later the dog was still just as afraid of the husband, to his deep sorrow.

    Accidents such as this can happen.

2. A Norwegian Elkhound had been at a dog show, and the judge had hurt her with the measuring stick whilst measuring her height. She became terrified of people, and would not let anyone near her. Fortunately the owner came to see me as soon as she could after the incident and we could start working on helping the dog straight away. Five months later she was herself again, and could go to another show to get her last ribbon, which she needed to be allowed by the breed club to have puppies and have them registered.

3. The owner of a Labrador was so scared that the dog should jump on and hurt children that when the dog wanted to approach them she yelled "NO" and jerked the dog back. In a very short time the dog went from loving children to hating them, and couldn't stand the sight of children at any distance.

Giving a negative association is possibly one of the most usual ways of teaching dogs to become angry at dogs and people – and it is so unnecessary. If you have a little knowledge about how learning by association works, it is so easy to avoid teaching the dog to develop a problem towards people and dogs. And it is so easy instead to just make a sound to make the dog pass the child, or teach him to sit nicely to say hello.

4. A dog and owner were participating in a class. During the training session, which was too long and strenuous, the dog became thirsty. Whilst passing a water bowl he went over to it for a drink. The instructor spotted that, and threw himself at the dog, yelling "NOOOOO" at the top of his voice.

    The dog startled, and did not dare to drink. He did not dare to drink when he got home either. When the owners contacted me two days later, the dog had still not dared to drink, and was on the verge of collapse.

    He could easily have died. This was such unnecessary suffering for a dog who simply wanted to drink when he was thirsty.

We must learn to think about how we do things. A simple wrong action on our part can have far-reaching consequences. So many dogs today are put down because of the mistakes we make.

Mistakes are made not only by dog owners but by instructors and trainers who ought to know better.

General examples

You are teaching your dog to retrieve. When he picks up the dumbbell and begins to mouth it, you shout "No!" You mean: "don't chew", but the dog in most cases associates your "no" with having the dumbbell in his mouth. He spits it out, and subsequently becomes scared of picking it up. Many a good retrieve exercise has been destroyed this way.

If you say "NO" every time a puppy chews something out of curiosity he will soon learn that it is dangerous to have something in his mouth – and you may get greater problems later in the dog's life if you want this dog to retrieve.

A friend of mind got a dog when it was four years old. The dog did not dare have anything in her mouth. No toys, no chew bones, absolutely nothing unless it was her food. The owner wanted the dog to retrieve as we were having lots of fun with searching and finding objects.

It took the dog three years to get over the fear, and even then nobody could even look at her when she did it. If they did, she would drop it immediately.

All because she had been told "NO, NO, NO" all the time as a puppy.

Pulling on leash also creates negative associations for the dog

Reminders

How to teach your dog to walk nicely:

It is best to start teaching the dog a neutral sound first.

Do this at home or in a quiet place. Stand still, make the sound, praise and reward IMMEDIATELY the dog turns towards the sound. Repeat a few times. You will see how quickly your dog understands that the noise indicates a treat.

Wait until the dog turns towards you, then immediately reward the response

Next:

Make the sound, praise the dog when he turns, walk a couple of steps away, then reward. (See figs. 7, 8 and 9)

When this begins to work well, you can start doing this several times in a row, by changing direction 3-4 times. Make the sound first, then walk away when the dog looks your way, reward, make the sound again, and repeat the procedure.

Fig. 7

It is often easiest to train in a quiet place with no distractions

Fig. 8

Fig. 9

When this works well, put a leash on the dog and do the same thing. Be absolutely sure that you have a loose leash. Look again at the pictures in this book and see how slack the leash is. Yours should be like that too.

When both you and your dog can do this with ease inside your home, in the garden or in another quiet place, this is the time to go out and meet the occasional distraction. However, ensure that there are not many distractions in the beginning, and that they are some distance away. If they are too close increase the distance to ensure that your dog can succeed.

When you and your dog are good at this, and when you are good at keeping your leash slack, start rewarding a little less. Every second or third time, perhaps – but vary it a little so that your dog doesn't begin to predict when the treat will come. The goal is to give a treat "every now and then" – but you should never cut out the treat completely. A variable schedule gives the best possible performance.

What is the point
of pulling on leash
if no one follows?

A slack leash
gives a much
better feeling!

Summary

Dogs often pull to the side when something is of interest. Allow the dog to explore a little, then use your sound to get him to follow you instead

1. Stop giving negative messages to your dog like yelling, pinching his ears, shaking the dog by the neck, saying NO or any other punishment when the dog is pulling.

2. Teach the dog to respond to a neutral signal to get his attention (but don't use eye contact!)

3. Start walking a few steps way from him to encourage him to follow.

4. Practise the same exercise on a leash, but ensure the leash is hanging loose.

5. Gradually start to walk in new places where there are more distractions

6. Reward the dog less frequently

7. Start using this technique in a wider variety of situations where you need the dog to move away from things, to pass or just to leave things alone.

8. Remember that walking nicely does NOT mean heeling, with the dog stuck to your side. The dog should be able to walk on the left or right, behind you or in front of you; he should be able to sniff and look around – but he should not pull.

9. Check the equipment you are using and ensure it is comfortable. Check your dog's health if necessary, and also work on the dog's development in social skills.

10. If the dog forgets himself and lunges or pulls, just stop, stand still for a few seconds. Then use the signal for attention again.

    It is natural for a dog to be curious. There is no need to punish a dog for something that feels so completely natural to him.

    You can avoid the pull or the lunge by using the sound for attention BEFORE the dog is actually pulling or lunging. If you are quick enough, you can prevent it from happening before it occurs.

A little practice and your dog will soon be responding nicely

Comments

Sally Askew, Rainbow Pet-Dog Training School, England:
With reference to a summer camp in Hardraw, Yorkshire

Turid's message is very powerful; simple yet at the same time so subtle. Her approach is startlingly unique. No one else… has her approach to dogs. It is a holistic approach, encouraging owners to look at the world from the dog's point of view.

Turid is a firm believer in teaching the art of the "loose leash" to dog owners. She has her own simple but efficient approach to this, which she demonstrated and encouraged us to use. As with everything else Turid teaches, one simple tool has a multitude of benefits. In this case the method combines all the following:

- It teaches you how to get the dog's attention
- It reduces stress in the dog by reducing pressure on the neck
- It stops the dog pulling
- It reinforces the recall
- It teaches the owner how hard the dog has to concentrate in order to walk with you as well as being aware of everything else that is going on around
- It mentally stimulates the dog
- It allows the dog to use its own calming signals
- It can solve the problems of lunging, barking and of aggressive dogs on leash
- It also helps to calm the owner

All in all a very useful tool.

Sheila Harper:

Having used Turid's leash work method for some years with success with rescue dogs that already pulled on lead, I finally had the opportunity to see what would happen when training a puppy without any previous influences.

My Alaskan Malamute puppy was the chosen one! Taku would be a big boy when fully grown, and it would be important for him to learn not to pit his weight against mine.

Not only was the method quick, but also I soon found that just as the leash was about to tighten, he automatically adjusted himself so there was no pull at all.

Due to circumstances beyond my control Taku missed out on some crucial socialisation as an adolescent and became extremely excited about seeing other dogs. Most dogs lunge and lean into the lead. Taku didn't bother! It was so easy to make the orientation sound, get him to calmly turn towards me and to lead him away from the source of any distraction.

This training has remained with him ever since. At eight years of age he is a pleasure to walk.

I have tried out many methods of training dogs to walk on a slack lead. There is no doubt in my mind that Turid's research is right. This is the only method I've used that reduces stress in both dog and owner, allows the dog to make the right choice, and allows the use of calming signals. Result: a very happy dog, and a very happy owner!

A few years ago, at a camp in the hills of Yorkshire, we were taking a walk together, and I had the privilege to have Taku on the leash (not many are allowed to!) Round a bend, on a narrow path, we were suddenly in the middle of chaos. Sheep on the left, only one metre away, cattle on the right side, just as close. And I wonder if any dog would have kept calm then. Taku did not. He bellowed and barked and made all the scary noises a Malamute can make, jumping up and down and lunging to the left and right. All on a totally loose leash! I was just standing there, with a loose leash and a hysterical dog on the other end, and I must admit that I enjoyed the whole thing! It was so utterly remarkable!

We got out of the situation easily, and it is one of my dearest memories from that lovely summer in the Yorkshire Dales.

Turid

Turid and Star

Afterthoughts

My wish would be to live in a society where dogs are respected and treasured for what they are.

It would be a place where dogs are walked at leisure on harness and a loose leash along roads with traffic, and off leash in parks and woods and fields. No shouting or irritation, only a pleasant and friendly atmosphere between dog and owner – and other people. Nobody jerking or hauling dogs along, but letting them sniff the smells they find interesting and allowing them to look at things that are happening around them.

How nice and relaxing that sounds! It **is** possible and within reach. It only takes a little thinking and understanding on our part, and it needs only a minimum of work.

Start planning your training now and do it carefully. Don't go too fast or demand too much of your dog. Decide to become your dog's best friend – and he will automatically become yours. Dogs do not think about revenge or bear grudges.

Consider the following:

Do not be so concerned about teaching your dog so much obedience. Instead, think about and develop your relationship with your dog – the rest will follow by itself.

In teaching your dog to walk nicely on a loose leash and respecting his natural curiosity of the environment, your relationship with your best friend will develop and blossom.

About the author

Turid Rugaas has spent most of her life with animals. A former racehorse trainer, Turid has always known instinctively that kind methods are the most effective, and has worked in this manner with any animal coming into her care.

She is founder of Hagen Hundeskole in Norway, training dogs and their owners, and spends most of her time travelling around the world to deliver her message.

Best known for her work on calming signals, studied at the end of the 1980's along with a colleague, Ståle Ødegaard, Turid produced her first book in 1996, with a video following shortly afterwards.

Turid is a founder member and President of the Pet Dog Trainers of Europe, an organisation devoted to teaching through kindness and respect.

Turid and Saga

Bibliography

*Roger Abrantes	Evolution of Canine Social Behaviour
Åsa Ahlbom / Agneta Geneborg	Rasekunnskap
Ted Baer	How To Teach an Old Dog New Tricks
Bergljot Børresen	Kunsten å Bli Tam Den Ensomme Apen
*Suzanne Clothier	Bones Would Rain From the Sky
*Raymond & Lorna Coppinger	Dogs
*Jean Donaldson	The Culture Clash Dogs are From Neptune
Ian Dunbar	Dog Behaviour Good Little Dog Book
*Barry Eaton	Dominance – Fact or Fiction
Morten Egtvedt / Cecilie Køste	Klikkertrening For Din Hund
*Cindy Engel	Wild Health
*John Fisher	Dogwise Think Dog!
Lars Fält	Beteende Hundens Språk Och Flockliv

*Graham & Vlamis   Bach Flower Remedies for Animals

Mickie Gustafson   Valpen
                        Unghunden

Anders Halgren   Lexicon I Hundespråk
                        Hundens Gyllene Regler
                        Rückenprobleme

Silvia Hartmann-Kent   Training Your Dog with Love

*Roy Hunter   Fun Nosework For Dogs

Konrad Lorenz   Man Meets Dog
                        On Aggression

*Patricia McConnell   Cautious Canine
                        The Other End of The Leash

*Jeffrey Mason   When Elephants Weep

David Mech   articles 1999 – 2002

*James O'Heare   The Canine Aggression Workbook
                        The Canine Separation
                        Anxiety Workbook

*Karen Pryor   Don't Shoot the Dog
                        Lads Before the Wind

*Pamela Reid   Excel-erated Learning

*Terry Ryan   The Toolbox for Remodelling
                        Problem Dogs

*Linda Tellington Jones   Get in Ttouch With Your Dog

Daniel Tortora   Right Dog For You

Weston and Ross   Dog Problems – the Gentle
                          Modern Cure

Morgan Spector   Clicker Training for Obedience

Nicole Wilde   So You Want to Be a Dog Trainer

*Books by these authors are also available from the extensive mail order section of dog-related books, videos, accessories and training equipment at:

Sheila Harper Canine Education
9 The Meadows
Rugeley
Staffs WS15 1JH
England

Tel: + 44 (0) 1889 802 685
email: sheila@qanuk.com
www.qanuk.com

By the same author

Book – On Talking Terms With Dogs: Calming Signals by Turid Rugaas

Turid Rugaas' revolutionary work incorporates what is probably the single most important study of canine social language. Turid has been observing and analysing calming signals for years; she has documented over 30 signals and presents her findings in this book, along with photographic illustrations and explanations and of why and how they are used. By studying these signals and improving our powers of observation we can increase our ability to communicate with our dogs.

If you have ever wondered what your dog is trying to tell you then this is the book for you!

Revised/updated with new material and colour photographs.

Video & DVD – Calming Signals: What Your Dog Tells You by Turid Rugaas

The companion to Turid's best selling book: On Talking Terms With Dogs is now available on both video and DVD. Turid presents us with a unique opportunity to see footage of dogs using calming signals, increasing our own ability to study and observe the signals. Turid, who is the foremost authority in the world on dog language, gives explanations and shows us how we can use calming signals in our own interactions with dogs. Become an addictive dog-watcher with this fascinating, compulsive viewing.

Now you too can truly be "on talking terms with dogs"!

Viewing time: approximately 45 minutes. Some new footage also included. Video in PAL format for British/European VCRs.

62

Pet Dog Trainers of Europe

The PDTE is a growing organisation devoted to educating dogs and owners through kindness and respect. A co-founder and President of the PDTE, Turid has tirelessly promoted the principles behind it, concerning herself with the general welfare of dogs world-wide.

Through the PDTE it is hoped to promote the best possible practices in dog ownership, handling and training, thereby advancing the well-being of dogs throughout the world.

The PDTE was set up to:

- develop and extend our understanding of how dogs see the world and how they communicate with each other and with humans

- gain a greater understanding of ways that we can develop a positive relationship between dogs and people

Aims of the PDTE

The PDTE aims to encourage mambership by anyone who has a relationship with dogs with the aim of living in harmony, engendering mutual respect and giving people the desire and responsibility to be considerate of both social groups.

For further information please visit the website:

www.pet-dog-trainers-europe.com

Membership application forms are available from Sheila Harper (Secretary PDTE). Contact details are on the following page.

Further information

For further information on any of the following please find contact details below:

- to order further titles by Turid
- for information on her courses, to study her methods or to attend other courses based on her work
- for information relating to the Pet Dog Trainers of Europe
- for dog-related books and videos by other authors, along with accessories and training equipment

please contact:

Sheila Harper Canine Education
9 The Meadows, Rugeley, Staffs. WS15 1JH England
Tel: 0044 (0)1889 802 685
email: sheila@qanuk.com
website: www.qanuk.com